EUGENE BOZZA

BALLADE
for Bass Clarinet & Piano

PIANO

Dédié aux Clarinettistes: R.M. Avey, J. E. Elliott, M. Fossenkemper,
E. Schmachtenberg et G. E. Waln.

BALLADE
For Bass Clarinet and Piano
(Original Version)

SS-287

EUGENE BOZZA

2

Ballade - 6

EUGENE BOZZA

BALLADE
for Bass Clarinet & Piano

Bass Clarinet in Bb

Dédié aux Clarinettistes: R. M. Arey, J. E. Elliott, M. Fossenkemper,
E. Schmachtenberg et G. E. Waln.

BALLADE
For Bass Clarinet and Piano
(Original Version)

BASS CLARINET in B♭

EUGENE BOZZA

Bass Clarinet in B♭

SS-287

Ballade

Paris July 14 - 1939

Selected Bass/ Contra-Bass Clarinet Publications

METHODS

RHOADS, WILLIAM

B217   21 Foundation Studies (Grade 4)   HL3770300

B110   35 Technical Studies (Grade 4)   HL3770187

These technical studies have been compiled in an effort to give the alto and bass clarinetists "their own" material for study. They are intended to provide alto and bass clarinetists with the same technical facility as other instruments in the clarinet family.

B216   Etudes for Technical Facility (Grade 3)   HL3770299

WEISSENBORN, JULIUS

Rhoads, William

B256   Advanced Studies (Grade 5)   HL3770370

One of the most widely used collections of studies for the advancing player/student of the Alto and/or Bass Clarinets.

COLLECTIONS

RHOADS, WILLIAM

B447   Ten Solos for Concert and Contest (Grade 4)   HL3770635

I. Fantasy, II. Adagio and Allegro, III. Caprice, IV. Tarantella, V. A Minor Tune, VI. Piece in G Minor, VII. Allegretto in C Minor, VIII. Andante and Allegro, IX. Scherzando, X. Nocturne

SOLO WITH PIANO

BOZZA, EUGENE

SS287   Ballade (Grade 3)   HL3773914

This piece uses shifting tonalities in both scalar and arpeggiated sections to great effect throughout. It is a wonderful recital or contest piece for the intermediate to advancing bass clarinet player.

CAILLIET, LUCIEN

ST221   Le Pionnier (The Pioneer) (Grade 3)   HL3774832

This piece, written for contrabass Clarinet, can also be played on bass clarinet.

DAVIS, WILLIAM MAC

ST441   Variations on a Theme Of Robert Schumann   HL3775128
            (Grade 3)

Concert band accompaniment also published by Southern Music. (S537CB)

DESPORTES, YVONNE

SS148   Andante and Allegro (Grade 3)   HL3773752

GALLIARD, JOHANN ERNST

Merriman, Lyle

SS686   Adagio and Allegro (Grade 3)   HL3774337

MARCELLO, BENEDETTO

Hite, David

SS159   Sonata in a Minor (Grade 3)   HL3773764

MARTY, GEORGES

Bonade/ Andraud

SS141   First Fantasie (Grade 5)   HL3773745

This was composed for the Paris National Conservatory Contest in 1897. Using Daniel Bonade's version for soprano clarinet, this edition for bass clarinet was transcribed by Albert Andraud.

RITTER, REINHOLD

Shanley, Richard

SU400   Long, Long Ago Op 12 (Grade 4)   HL3776309

"Long, Long Ago: Fantasie" (Lang, lang, ist's her") is a wonderful selection for the advancing player looking for a contest or recital piece that offers four progressive variations with distinctly contrasting styles. Versions for the standard Bb clarinet, Eb clarinet, Eb alto/contra alto clarinet, and Bb Bass/ Contrabass clarinet are available from the publisher.

SENAILLE, JEAN BAPTISTE

Ephross, Arthur

ST360   Allegro Spiritoso (Grade 3)   HL3775018

The "Allegro Spiritoso" is the 3rd movement of a Sonata in D Minor. Versions for following instruments are available from the publisher: alto clarinet, bass clarinet, contra alto clarinet, contrabass clarinet, alto saxophone, tenor saxophone, baritone saxophone, bassoon, euphonium/trombone, and tuba.

SENAILLE, JEAN BAPTISTE

Thurston, Richard

SU114   Allegro Spiritoso (Grade 3)   HL3775933

The "Allegro Spiritoso" is the 3rd movement of a Sonata in D Minor. This arrangement can also be performed on a Bb bass clarinet. Versions for following instruments are available from the publisher: alto clarinet, bass clarinet, contra alto clarinet, contrabass clarinet, alto saxophone, tenor saxophone, baritone saxophone, bassoon, euphonium/trombone, and tuba.

SOLOMON, EDWARD

ST915   Gypsy Song (Grade 3)   HL3775773

This lively tune in harmonic minor provides the perfect vehicle for the beginning soloist. Versions for both Bb and Eb low clarinets are available from the publisher.

Exclusively distributed by HAL•LEONARD CORPORATION

Questions/ comments? info@laurenkeisermusic.com

5

6

Allegro vivo

Paris July 14- 1939